NICK FAWCETT

W0009155

Beginnings and Endings
A LENT STUDY BOOK

First published in 2005 by

KEVIN MAYHEW LTD
Buxhall, Stowmarket, Suffolk, IP14 3BW
E-mail: info@kevinmayhew.com
www.kevinmayhew.com

9 8 7 6 5 4 3 2 1 0

ISBN 1 84417 491 3
Catalogue No. 1500859

Cover illustration by Angela Palfrey
Cover design by Angela Selfe
Edited and typeset by Katherine Laidler

Printed and bound in Great Britain

Contents

To John and Mary Ackland
remembering with gratitude
your support during my student ministry

Introduction

One of my all-time favourite hymns is the Sydney Carter classic 'One more step along the world I go'. The words neatly encapsulate the idea of faith being an ongoing journey, a lifelong pilgrimage in which each day offers a fresh start, unexplored possibilities. The first line of the chorus, in particular, says it all: 'So it's from the old I travel to the new'. What, though, do we mean by such talk? What is it as Christians we see ourselves leaving behind, and in what way does life bring new beginnings, a break with the past leading to a transformed present and future full of promise? The language strikes a chord deep within, but how seriously do we consider what it means? Lent offers an ideal opportunity to do just that, for, with its emphasis on contrition and self-denial, coupled with the events of the Passion and resurrection that it anticipates, it perhaps has more to say than any other season about both beginnings and endings in relation to Christian commitment.

In this study book I approach those twin points from three paired perspectives. Sessions 1 and 2 look at the idea of moving from the old self to the new, or, to put it another way, of turning from one way of life to another. What does this involve in practice? What aspects of our life need to be ended and what new characteristics put in their place? Is this transition a one-off event or an ongoing process, and, if the latter, can that process be obstructed, even put into reverse? Session 3 takes us to what, for many, is the central theme of this season – the practice of giving something up for Lent – a theme balanced in the fourth session by asking whether in fact Lent is a time to take things on. The last two sessions look towards Holy Week and Easter, exploring in turn what God has decisively achieved for us through the death and resurrection of Christ, and the new beginnings this makes possible, in this life and the next.

Throughout the preparation of this book I have wrestled with one of the fundamental issues of Christian doctrine – the relationship of faith and works – the tension between the two being thrown up time and time again. I cannot claim to have resolved it satisfactorily, certainly not to have come up with a cohesive and consistent synthesis. I am no systematic theologian, nor can I claim any hotline to God – rather, I am a fellow-pilgrim with you, the reader, daily searching for deeper understanding and a fuller faith. My hope is that something in these pages will stir thought and provoke discussion to bring such faith and understanding a little closer. Above all, I hope that you will find reflecting on Lent as challenging yet rewarding an experience as I have.

NICK FAWCETT

Session 1
Off with the old . . .

Opening music

Sing together, or play a recording of, the hymn 'Dear Lord and Father of mankind'.

Setting the scene

'Dear Lord and Father of mankind, forgive our foolish ways' – we'll all, I'm sure, have echoed those words countless times in our lives, like the Apostle Paul chafing with frustration at our inability to honour God as we would wish. We mean to put aside former ways, but it proves easier said than done. So what exactly does it mean to put off the old self, and how do we go about it? Those are the sort of questions we will be exploring in this first session.

Opening prayer

Mighty God,
    through our meeting here with one another
    may we meet also with you,
    hearing your voice,
    and responding to your living and active word.
Search our hearts and open our minds,
    so that in the light of your truth and faithfulness
    we may recognise those areas of life where we fail you,
    acknowledging our faults,
    confessing our weaknesses,
    and, in your mercy, finding grace to start again,
    through Jesus Christ our Lord.
Amen.

Reading

Examine me, O God, and know what's in my heart; assess me and recognise what's in my mind. See if there is any misguided way within me, and lead me in your eternal path.
Psalm 139:23-24

First thoughts

Sackcloth and ashes, confession and repentance – those for many sum up what Lent is all about. It's a season that conjures up images of monks in hair shirts and ascetics mortifying the flesh – all very laudable, no doubt, but hardly the stuff of daily discipleship. Indeed, if it were, our commitment would swiftly start to pall. Not that we underestimate the importance of confession or feel we've nothing to repent of – far from it – but such austere practices smack of another age and seem to emphasise works rather than faith, as though we can somehow earn God's forgiveness rather than receive it through grace.

What place, then, does that leave for Lent today? Is it a relic of years gone by, having little if any place in modern society? Should we abandon its focus on contrition and penitence altogether, observing it instead simply as a time for prayer and reflection? Or can we use it positively rather than negatively as an opportunity to examine our lives, acknowledging where we are found wanting and taking steps to put things right?

In this session I want to approach the theme from the perspective of beginnings and endings, or, more accurately, old and new: the person we once were – and all too often still are – and the person we're called to be in Christ. That's a subject on which the Apostle Paul in particular has much to say, as we will see in a moment.

Group activity

'Past history' (see Appendix 1)

Music

'Have mercy on me, O God' from *In God alone* by Andrew Moore

Prayer of intercession

Merciful God,
    reach out to those who feel trapped by past mistakes,
    unable to shake off their former self and start again.
We pray for those racked by guilt or burdened by remorse –
    may they find freedom in the forgiveness you offer.
We pray for those who strive to change but despair of doing so,
    temptation proving too strong,
    the flesh too weak –
    may they find renewal through your transforming grace.
We pray for those whose errors have undermined relationships,
    destroying trust,
    provoking resentment,
    causing hurt in body, mind and soul –
    may your Spirit bring reconciliation.
We pray for victims of such hurt,
    those who have been left feeling betrayed,
    cheated,
    disillusioned
    or wounded by the wrongdoing of others –
    may your love bring healing.
Wherever the past holds captive,
    denying, dividing and destroying,
    lead on from the old to the new,
    through Jesus Christ our Lord.
Amen.

Readings

We know that our former self was put to death with Christ on the cross, so that the power of everything wrong within that old nature might be destroyed, releasing us from sin's bondage.
Romans 6:6

The person you used to be, your old self in other words, was being destroyed by its misplaced cravings. Get rid of it! And get rid similarly of all bitterness, rage, temper, backbiting and insults, together with all malice. Be kind to one another instead, compassionate, forgiving others as God in Christ has forgiven you.
Ephesians 4:22, 31-32

Put to death whatever is earthly within you: sexual immorality, depravity, indecency, lust and other evil desires, including greed, which is a form of idolatry, because the wrath of God will come on account of such things. You once followed ways such as these, in your former way of life, but now you must get rid of all such things – rage, anger, malice, slander, abusive language and deceitful behaviour, for you have renounced the old self with its associated practices.
Colossians 3:5-9

Further thoughts

Read the letters of Paul concerning how we should and shouldn't live, and we could be excused for feeling a touch smug. We're quite ready to admit we're far from perfect, but not even our worst enemies would associate us with the vices Paul typically comes up with – depravity, indecent behaviour, lust, drunken revelling, orgies and the like – such activities far removed from our daily lifestyles. In consequence, when Paul waxes lyrical – as he so often does – about the need to put off the old dissipated self with all its weaknesses, we automatically switch off, assuming that his words have nothing to say to us. Take, for example, the following passage from Romans, in which he rounds on the corruption of the Gentiles: 'Their lives are awash with all manner of vices and sin: evil and avarice, envy, murder, aggression, treachery and spite. They gossip about each other's faults, and treat God with utter contempt, being so full of themselves, so arrogant, that they actually take pride in devising new ways to flout his will' (Romans 1:29-31). Strong stuff indeed, but how far does it touch base with our day-to-day experience?

It would be a mistake, though, to ignore Paul altogether, assuming nothing in our lives needs changing, for look elsewhere at what he says about the old and new self and a great deal will almost certainly hit closer to home. Listen again, for example, to some of the traits he highlights in his words to the Ephesians and Colossians – and I mean *really* listen. Instead of allowing the words simply to wash over you, pause and ponder, asking yourself honestly and prayerfully how far these still have a place in your life: bitterness . . . rage . . . irritability . . . backbiting . . . insults . . . abusive language . . . spite. Do those ring any bells for you? I'd be surprised if they don't. If not though, try these for size: pride . . . envy . . . prejudice . . . intolerance . . . greed . . . selfishness . . . meanness . . . apathy. Are you still feeling smug? I'm not, for I know such things are still all too much a part of me. I wish they were consigned to the past – characteristics of some former self – but I'm well aware how readily they can surface, undermining my relationship with God and others.

But wait, you may say, enough of this morbid introspection. Surely the gospel is about God's forgiveness, the way he has dealt, through the grace of Christ, with whatever's wrong in our lives and made us new. And, as will emerge time and again in this book, you'd be absolutely right. Yet it's easy to abuse that truth, assuming that, since God will forgive anyway, it doesn't matter if we go astray. Paul himself was well aware of that danger. 'Are we to suggest,' he wrote, 'that it's all right to carry on with doing wrong since it gives God the opportunity to show even more mercy?' (Romans 6:1). His answer kicks the idea firmly into touch. 'Of course not! We've died to sin so how can we happily continue to live with it?' (Romans 6:2). Yes, we depend on grace, and, yes, the business of making us new is ultimately down to God, but that doesn't mean we have no part to play. Unless we're ready to take a long, hard look at ourselves, identifying where we fall short and genuinely looking to change, we tie his hands. Simply praying 'pardon my faults' is not enough, nor does it suffice merely to echo those words of the Psalmist: 'Examine me, O God, and know what's in my heart; assess me and recognise what's in my mind. See if there is any misguided way within me, and lead me in your eternal path' (Psalm 139:23-24). That may certainly secure forgiveness but if we're serious about changing, getting rid of what scars our dealings with God and those around us, then we need the courage to both recognise our faults and confess them, so that with God's help we can move on. That's what Lent invites us to do: honestly and prayerfully to reflect on who we are, to consider who we should be, and to seek his help in bridging the gap.

Prayer

Lord Jesus Christ,
    help us to examine ourselves, humbly and honestly,
    seeing ourselves as we really are.
Help us to face the truths we'd rather ignore,
    to admit those mistakes we're loath to own up to,
    to acknowledge those weaknesses we've pushed under the carpet,
    hoping they'll go away.
Give us the courage we need to confess our faults,
    so that you can work within us,
    transforming what *is* into what you would have it be.
Wherever the old self lives on within us,
    come now in your redeeming, restoring power
    and make us new.
Amen.

Music

'Miserere nobis, Domine' from *Awakening in Love* by Margaret Rizza

Meditation of a Christian in Galatia

We'd come together for one purpose that day –
    our little fellowship in Galatia –
    gathered expressly to listen to Paul's latest letter
    and hear what the great man had to say.
And, as his message unfolded,
    I have to say I was feeling pretty pleased,
    even, I admit, a touch smug,
    for while some around me squirmed
    at the mention of drunkenness,
    dissolution,
    debauchery,
    I could breathe easily,
    for no such skeletons lurked in my cupboard.
But if I seriously thought I had grounds for complacency
    I was in for a shock,
    for suddenly the words hit closer to home –
    far too close.
'Have nothing to do with rage,' he said,
    'get rid of anger' . . .
    and I felt the colour rise to my cheeks,
    for only that morning I'd lost my temper,
    shouting at the kids,
    and then picking a fight with the wife
    that had more to do with my pique
    than any wrongdoing on her part.
And there was more,
    much more:

envy, pride, avarice, selfishness, to name but some,
each all too much a part of me.
It was like standing in a hall of distorted glass
and seeing a grotesque caricature staring back at me,
what should have spoken of Christ hideously marred.
I'd condemned greed, yet hungered for more,
extolled humility, yet been full of my own importance,
preached sacrifice and self-denial, yet feathered my nest,
advocated forgiveness, yet been swift to find fault.
Sure, I avoided certain vices,
not even the thought of them entering my head,
let alone the deed,
but in plenty else I was found wanting.
I'd thought I was different,
even presumed to thank God I wasn't like the rest,
but I realise now I should thank him simply for this –
that his love is freely given,
not earned,
and that somehow, despite my faults,
he's able to take what I am
and shape what I shall be,
by his grace leading me forward from the old to the new.

Closing music

Sing together, or play a recording of, the hymn 'Come, let us sing of a wonderful love'.

Final thought

Come to my heart, O thou wonderful love,
come and abide,
lifting my life till it rises above
envy and falsehood and pride;
seeking to be
lowly and humble, a learner of thee.

Blessing

Gracious God,
 continue to shape our lives,
 taking what we are
 and directing what we might become,
 leading us each day from the old to the new,
 our past to *your* future.
Amen.

Session 2
. . . on with the new

Opening music

Sing together, or play a recording of, the hymn 'Breathe on me, Breath of God'.

Setting the scene

Breathe on me, Breath of God,
fill me with life anew,
that I may love what thou dost love,
and do what thou dost do.

At the heart of our faith is the idea of being made new, re-created, but, as the words of that lovely hymn remind us, we cannot achieve it ourselves. New beginnings come from God, by the grace of Christ and the power of the Spirit. Lose sight of that and we lose sight of everything.

Opening prayer

Redeeming God,
    touch this time by your grace,
    so that it may be more than a social get-together,
    more than an established routine
    and more than a comfortable discussion.
Through the words we read,
    the thoughts we share,
    the music we listen to
    and the prayers we offer,

16

break into our lives,
bringing an openness to your will,
a deeper sense of calling
and a closer walk with you,
leading to true growth in faith and love,
genuine renewal in body, mind and spirit,
to the glory of your name.
Amen.

Reading

Anyone united with Christ is a new creation; the old self has passed away in its entirety; everything is made new.
2 Corinthians 5:17

First thoughts

Did you ever watch the BBC series *Changing Rooms*? Its success led to a plethora of spin-offs, virtually every series on television for a time seeming to feature some sort of makeover. I usually give such programmes a miss, perhaps because my DIY skills are minimal, but with *Changing Rooms* it was a different story – I found it compulsive viewing from the start, finding something almost magical about the way an ordinary, even dingy room can be transformed in a couple of days into something chic, classical or trendy.

Imagine if we could do that not just with buildings but also with people. According to another TV series, *What Not To Wear*, we can do just that, women of all shapes and sizes being astonishingly transformed in these programmes – through nothing more than an astute selection of clothing (and a little help from the beautician) – from Cinderella to the belle of the ball. But, of course, we're still only talking about makeovers here, changing outer appearances rather than what's hidden deep within. A room can be made to look like Buckingham Palace yet be riddled with damp or dry rot.

A person can be done up to resemble an angel yet be anything *but* underneath. In such cases, beauty is indeed skin deep. How far, if at all, is it possible to change people deep within?

It's hard not to be sceptical, isn't it? Greed, hatred, bigotry and corruption continue to scar society, much as they have ever done, and war, violence, injustice and exploitation are just as much a part of our world. Human nature, it seems, is the same yesterday, today and tomorrow. And yet the Bible speaks of a change more radical than even the most idealistic of us would dare contemplate, of making an entirely fresh start, becoming a new person, being born again. This is no mere makeover we're talking about, a tinkering with appearances, but a re-creation, a transformation deep within. How is that possible? What does it involve? And what does God ask of us in bringing it about? Those are the questions we'll be considering further later in this session.

Group activity

'Beginnings and endings'(see Appendix 1)

Music

'Creator Spirit, come' from *Sacred Weave* by Keith Duke

Prayer of intercession

Transforming and redeeming God,
    reach out to those who, conscious of their faults,
    seek new beginnings,
    true change,
    a fresh start,
    and, in your mercy, grant renewal.
Reach out to those who, having heard your word,
    are wrestling with its challenge,

grappling with your call,
and, in your mercy, grant faith.
Reach out to those who, having made a commitment,
are starting out on the journey of discipleship,
yearning to live as your disciples,
and, in your mercy, grant guidance.
Reach out to all who, in this season of Lent,
are seeking deeper faith,
truer service,
rekindled commitment,
and, in your mercy, grant growth.
Bring new beginnings in the hearts and lives of all,
this and every day,
through Jesus Christ our Lord.
Amen.

Readings

Be renewed deep within, mind and soul, putting on the new self created in the likeness of God, in righteousness, holiness and truth. Be thoughtful and compassionate in all your dealings with each other, showing forgiveness just as God has done to you in Christ.
Ephesians 4:23-24, 32

You have become a new person, your minds being renewed into the likeness of the one who created you. So then, as God's chosen ones, holy and greatly loved, clothe yourselves with compassion, kindness, humility, meekness and patience, being merciful to one another and forgiving any quarrel you may have; in other words, forgive as the Lord forgave you. Above all, clothe yourselves with love, which binds everything together in perfect harmony.
Colossians 3:9b-10, 12-14

Further thoughts

Can we really become different people, moving from one way of life to another? The short answer is no. If we're talking about turning over a new leaf, then, try as we might, we will never fully succeed. We may accomplish much – witness the way people manage to quit smoking or the abuse of alcohol and drugs – willpower being something we should never underestimate, but a fundamental restructuring, complete overhaul, is quite simply beyond our reach. Yet what *we* can't do, *God can* – that's the emphatic assertion of the gospel. And he does so in two ways.

First, and almost paradoxically, he views us as made new even when we're not. In other words, even though our faults and failings continue to be all too apparent, he counts us, through the death of Christ, as forgiven, restored, made perfect by proxy. That's what it means to talk of grace: it's about complete and undeserved mercy, God doing what we alone can never do.

Yet that's not to say we can leave everything to him, as if the way we live is unimportant. God longs to see new beginnings in our lives, not for his benefit but for ours and that of those around us. He wants to see an end to whatever devalues life – hurting and harming, denying joy, obscuring hope and impeding fulfilment – and in its place he hungers to see qualities that enrich, enhance, bless, nurture, strengthen, support, comfort, heal. What sort of things are we talking about? Listen once more to some of the features Paul lists: thoughtfulness . . . compassion . . . forgiveness . . . humility . . . kindness . . . modesty . . . patience . . . righteousness . . . honesty . . . self-control . . . above all, love. Are those *really* a part of your life? Think about it, carefully, prayerfully, and ask yourself when you last exhibited such qualities. We will not acquire them through our own efforts, though it doesn't hurt to try, for unless we seek we will surely not find. They come, finally, through drawing closer to Christ, cultivating a rapport with him, reflecting on what he has said and done, and opening our hearts to what his Spirit *continues* to say and do today.

We all fall short, and always will. Acknowledge that, yes, but don't punish yourself over it, for remember, God accepts you as you are, not for what you might become. Lent is a time for penitence but not penance; a time, most of all, simply for clothing ourselves more fully with Christ, who alone can make all things new.

Prayer

Redeeming God,
    take our desire to change,
    our yearning to be more like Jesus,
    and, by your grace, do what we can never hope to achieve
    alone.
Take what we are
    and fashion what we shall be,
    clothing us with love, joy and peace,
    with garments of humility, patience, honesty and compassion –
    qualities that will speak for themselves,
    testifying not to any merit of our own
    but to your renewing power and transforming grace.
Deepen our knowledge of you,
    our relationship with Christ
    and our openness to your Spirit,
    so that you may work your miracle of love within us,
    bringing us a fraction closer each day
    to becoming the people you already count us to be,
    through Jesus Christ our Lord.
Amen.

Meditation of one of Paul's companions

He wasn't much to look at, Paul,
   just an ordinary bloke, really,
   plain,
   even dull.
Yet when I met him I was spellbound,
   unable to tear myself away.
He had an aura that held you transfixed,
   fascinated,
   and, above all, humbled;
   a charisma, dare I say it, that spoke of Christ,
   embodying his love and goodness,
   as if Jesus himself were living through him.
No, I wasn't simply in awe of his reputation,
   and I'm not suggesting he suddenly sprouted wings and a halo.
He had his faults like the rest of us –
   a tad tetchy,
   occasionally severe,
   often stubborn,
   and, if you can count it as a vice, long-winded to a fault!
Yet he was also thoughtful,
   caring,
   unassuming,
   patient,
   always ready to listen
   and equally to forgive,
   his love for others breathtaking,
   unlike anything I've seen before.
And most special of all is that he didn't know it,
   nothing in his manner smacking for a moment
   of self-righteousness,
   still less of smug superiority.
He counted himself the chief of sinners and least of Apostles,
   can you believe that!
And he was constantly seeking to grow,

to become more like the one he loved and served –
    clothed with Christ.
Well, if you ask me he got as close as anyone,
    his life shining like a star in a dark and crooked world.
Yes, he was plain outwardly,
    and as for his dress sense, let's be kind and call it uninspired,
    but I tell you this,
    had he been dressed in rags he would still have been clothed
    in splendour,
    for in those qualities he wore with such distinction,
    those garments of compassion, humility, mercy and love,
    are clothes without equal,
    robes fit for a king.

Closing music

Sing together, or play a recording of, the hymn 'Love divine, all
loves excelling'.

Final thought

Finish, then, thy new creation:
pure and spotless let us be;
let us see thy great salvation,
perfectly restored in thee;
changed from glory into glory,
till in heaven we take our place,
till we cast our crowns before thee,
lost in wonder, love and praise.

Blessing

Lord Jesus Christ,
    go with us now,
    and nurture each day
    the seeds of life you have sown in our hearts,
    so that, despite everything that threatens to choke
    and destroy them,
    they may grow within us,
    reaching upwards and outwards
    and producing a rich harvest of spiritual fruit,
    to your glory.
Amen.

Session 3
Giving it up

Opening music

Play a recording, if you can get hold of it, of the opening lines of the 1982 hit single 'T'aint what you do, it's the way that you do it'.

Setting the scene

When Bananarama and Fun Boy Three released that song way back in 1982 I'm sure the last thing they had in mind was the season of Lent, yet their words are curiously appropriate to our theme today, taking us succinctly to a distinction between what we do and how we do it. As we will see, that difference is vital when it comes to considering the value or otherwise of giving something up to mark this season.

Opening prayer

Gracious God,
    in this season of Lent give us a deeper understanding
    of how you would have us live
    and of how best we can honour you.
Teach us more of Christ
    and what it means to take up our cross and walk in his footsteps.
So may we grow in faith, love and service,
    to the glory of your name.
Amen.

Readings

If any want to come after me, let them deny themselves and take up their cross daily, and then follow me. For those wishing to save their life will lose it, but those who lose their life for my sake will save it. All those who fail to take up their cross and walk in my footsteps are unworthy to be my disciples.
Luke 9:23-24; Matthew 10:38

Think twice before making a public show of religious devotion aimed at impressing others, for if you do that you will deny yourself any reward from your heavenly Father. Whenever you make a donation to the needy, for example – whether in the synagogue or out in the street – don't copy the hypocrites, who blow their own trumpet, eager to milk the plaudits. Mark my words, they have received the only reward they are going to get. Instead, when you make charitable gifts, ensure that one hand has no idea what the other is doing; your giving, in other words, should be known only to you; and your Father, who sees what is going on in the heart, will reward you . . . Similarly, whenever you fast, don't emulate the hypocrites by deliberately putting on a long face and pained expression to ensure that everyone knows all about your fast. I repeat, the only reward such people can look forward to is the one they've already enjoyed. By contrast, when you fast, spruce yourselves up as you would for a feast, anointing your head with oil and washing your face, so that the only one who knows you are fasting is your Father, who knows your innermost thoughts and will reward you accordingly.
Matthew 6:1-4; 6:16-18

First thoughts

What are you giving up for Lent? That question, and the idea implicit within it, sums up what for many, both inside and outside the Church, this season is all about – a time of sacrifice and self-

26

denial; of fasting for the true ascetic, and for the rest of us, if nothing else, of giving up life's little luxuries – chocolates, cream cakes, and so forth. But why do that? What, if anything, is it meant to achieve? For some the motivation is purely prosaic, Lent offering an ideal opportunity to follow a long-intended diet, give up smoking, cut down on alcohol or control an unruly temper – in other words, to get rid of some unwelcome vice or weakness. For others the aim is religious, predominantly to express remorse and penitence, to cultivate self-discipline, to respond to the poor, or simply to identify with the forty days and nights that Jesus spent in the wilderness, denying himself food or other material comforts as he wrestled with temptation and the nature of his calling. Such goals may be well intended, but do they really capture the spirit of Lent or, more important, of the gospel itself? The answer to that is well expressed in the song we heard earlier, for when it comes to sacrifice and self-denial, perhaps more than anywhere, it's not what we do but the way we do it that matters most, or, perhaps more accurately, *why* we do it.

Let me give you an example. If I were to rush out today and buy my wife an expensive bouquet of flowers with the sole purpose of saying, 'I love you', she'd be thrilled to bits. The gift would be special, not because of what it cost me but simply for what it said. If, however, I bought the flowers because I wanted something in return, or was nursing a guilty conscience, or felt it was my duty to do so, the gift would immediately be tarnished, devalued to the point of being worthless. The motivation is everything. So it is with giving something up for God. As Jesus observed in relation to fasting or giving alms to the poor, a deed can appear devout yet spring from entirely the wrong motives, being more about parading our virtue than concern for others, about winning plaudits than offering worship. What looks like selfless sacrifice can be altogether different: an attempt to salve one's conscience, earn God's blessing or avert his anger; or, indeed, it may be offered simply out of duty, given because we must, rather than because we may. The danger is as real for us as it was for the scribes and

Pharisees, self-denial, though we would never admit it, becoming a means of self-service or of twisting God's arm. If that's what Lent has become for you – and consider that possibility carefully before dismissing it too readily – then, quite honestly, you're better off forgetting it, for it's become more about you than him – about your guilt than his grace, your wishes than his purpose, your fear than his love.

Group activity

'Giving it up' (see Appendix 1)

Music

'Take, Lord' from *Awakening in Love* by Margaret Rizza

Prayer of intercession

Lord Jesus Christ,
    remembering how you freely surrendered your all,
    so we remember now those who, in love, make sacrifices in turn.

We pray for those who give up jobs, homes, even relationships
    to care for loved ones:
    sacrificing so much through devotion to parents, partners,
    children or relations.
Encourage, support, strengthen and equip them.

We pray for those who, in response to your call,
    give up the pursuit of wealth, comfort and prospects,
    offering themselves to the work of your kingdom
    through ministry, mission and evangelism,
    or through serving with charities and caring agencies
    at home and abroad.
Inspire, guide, enable and prosper them.

We pray for those who give up time and energy
in ways we take for granted,
freely offering their service in our churches, schools, hospitals
and all manner of voluntary services,
their practical work and support so often unsung
and yet so vital.
Bless, enthuse, lead and sustain them.

Hear our prayer for all who deny themselves
for the benefit of others,
and work through them to show your love
and share your blessing.
Amen.

Reading

If I dispense all my goods, and surrender my body to be burned,
yet do not have love, it is of no value to me whatsoever. Love is
patient and kind; it is not jealous or puffed up with its own
importance, vaunting itself before others, nor does it knowingly
cause offence. It does not seek its own well-being, is not easily
provoked, and does not think evil or rejoice in wrongdoing but
rejoices rather in the truth. It embraces all things, believes all
things, hopes all things, endures all things.
1 Corinthians 13:3-7

Further thoughts

Is there no place, then, for Lenten self-denial? Some would say
not, arguing that it smacks too much of works rather than faith, of
us taking the initiative rather than responding to *God's* grace. I
understand that concern full well, yet feel it is too sweeping,
personal sacrifice having a valid, even central place in discipleship as long as it is properly understood. Did not Jesus himself
say, *'when* you fast', rather than 'if', implying that he thought

such a practice a perfectly natural part of devotion? In almost the same breath, however, he goes on to talk of giving alms – in other words, of responding to the poor. To me this points to a link between giving something up and simply giving, self-denial affording an ideal opportunity to contribute meaningfully to others – not as a way of currying God's favour but as a response to his goodness, a grateful acknowledgement of all we've received.

Just think of the difference it would make if every Christian in this country lived frugally throughout Lent, giving the money saved to charity. What a sum could be raised and what an impact it could have on so many lives. Instead of having negative connotations, self-denial would become something positive – about affirming others, an expression of love.

This isn't, of course, the only argument that could be raised in support of sacrifice and self-denial, but it's a good one, worth pondering, I'd have thought. We're so good as Christians at extolling love, compassion and generosity, but how often do we practise it? We talk blithely of putting self last and others first, but does the way we live lend credence to such words? Lent offers a wonderful opportunity to put our money where our mouth is, practising what we preach and showing we really care. Perhaps, after all, it's worth asking, 'What are you giving up for Lent?'

Prayer

Merciful God,
    help us to use this season wisely,
    so that it may be a time of true growth and genuine service.
Save us from gesture religion,
    a parading of our virtue disguised as spiritual sacrifice.
Save us from empty show,
    self-denial aimed at seeking reward
    rather than expressing true love for you and others.

Teach us to seek your kingdom and your righteousness,
    putting aside whatever shuts you out or keeps us from you,
    and so, in letting go, may we grasp you more firmly,
    through Jesus Christ our Lord.
Amen.

Music

'Silent, surrendered' from *Fountain of Life* by Margaret Rizza

Meditation of a Pharisee, reflecting back on the Sermon on the Mount

I hate to say it, but he was right,
    his analysis of true worship and sacrifice spot on.
I'd fasted often
    and given generously,
    even going short on occasions myself,
    but commendable though it all seemed,
    dedicated,
    devout,
    it was chiefly about *me*,
    for my benefit as much as any.
I'd *intended* to serve God,
    and for a time thought I had,
    but though I didn't exactly trumpet it,
    I made quite sure others knew of my zeal in charity,
    constancy in devotion
    and steadfastness in self-denial.
And there was more, besides,
    for even my *unseen* acts of devotion were tarnished,

31

offered simply to bask in the glow of having done my bit,
    or in the expectation of material reward.
Hearing Jesus, however, brought home that piety is not enough,
    for God looks beneath the surface,
    into the heart and mind,
    assessing not only what we do but also why we do it,
    the thought as well as the action,
    and by that yardstick, I fear, I was measured and found wanting.
'So what now?' I hear you ask.
Will I still fast,
    still deny myself,
    still give to others?
Certainly I will,
    but out of love this time,
    joy instead of duty,
    and as to where and when,
    let alone how much or what,
    don't ask me that,
    or at least don't expect an answer if you do,
    for I've learned that some things are between me and him,
    and are far best staying that way.

Closing music

Sing together, or play a recording of, the hymn 'O thou who camest from above'.

Final thought

O thou who camest from above
the pure, celestial fire to impart,
kindle a flame of sacred love
on the mean altar of my heart.

Blessing

Take what we are, Lord,
    our living and giving,
    our caring and sharing,
    and use all to enrich our faith
    and to reach out in your name.
Amen.

Session 4
Taking it on

Opening music

Sing together, or play a recording of, the hymn 'Take my life and let it be'.

Setting the scene

Take my life, and let it be
consecrated, Lord, to thee:
take my moments and my days,
let them flow in ceaseless praise.

At first sight those words may seem to continue the theme of our last session – giving something up – but look more closely and we see that they actually say the opposite. They speak of consecrating every part of life, serving God through all we are and do; not so much of what we can't do as what we can.

Opening prayer

Loving God,
   inspire us, today and every day,
   through all you have done for us,
   to give something back to you,
   not in any attempt to repay the debt
   or to earn your blessing,
   but simply to say thank you for all we have received
   and gladly to share it.

Show us where and when we can most usefully respond,
   and use what we offer for your kingdom,
   through Jesus Christ our Lord.
Amen.

Readings

When the Son of Man comes in his glory, together with his angels,
he will sit in state on his throne, with all the nations gathered
before him, and he will separate people one from the other as a
shepherd separates the sheep from the goats, putting the sheep to
his right and the goats to his left. Then the king will say to those
on his right, 'Come, those whom my Father has blessed – inherit
the kingdom prepared for you from the foundation of the world. I
was hungry and you gave me something to eat, thirsty and you
gave me a drink, a stranger and you made me welcome, naked
and you clothed me, sick and you visited me, in prison and you
had time for me.' Then the righteous will answer, 'Lord, when did
we see you hungry and give you food, or thirsty and give you a
drink? When did we see you a stranger and make you welcome,
or naked and clothe you? When was it that we saw you sick or in
prison and visited you?' Then the king will answer, 'I tell you the
truth, whenever you did it to the least of your brothers and sisters,
you did it also to me.'
Matthew 25:31-40

If anyone decides to sue you and take your coat, offer your cloak
as well, and if someone forces you to go one mile, go a second
also. Give to whoever begs, and do not turn away anyone wishing
to borrow from you.
Matthew 5:40-42

First thoughts

Look in a mirror and what do you see? The answer, of course, is your own reflection staring back at you. Or at least it is but for one thing: the image is inverted, meaning that every feature you consider to be on your right side appears to others on your left, and vice versa. Anyone doubting that need only look at a piece of writing in a mirror to confirm the truth, the reflected 'words' seeming complete gobbledegook.

I remember much the same happening in my first attempt during college days to read a Hebrew Bible. As any Westerner would do, I automatically turned to the first page and attempted to read from left to right, as a result ending up utterly bamboozled, for Hebrew, of course, is a completely different language to our own, being read from right to left!

Do we during Lent, I wonder, through our focus on giving things up, similarly approach things the wrong way round? Consider, for a moment, the time Jesus spent in the wilderness. What mattered most there? Yes, the fasting and other privations were important, but surely most significant of all was what he took on during that time, committing himself to a path that would lead inexorably to the trauma of Gethsemane and agony on a cross. The wilderness experience, in other words, was above all one of accepting and responding to God's call – and it is precisely that which Jesus urged throughout his subsequent ministry. Yes, sacrifice is part of discipleship, not least the call to take up our cross and follow, but the emphasis of Jesus' preaching and teaching was consistently on going the extra mile, doing not just what's asked or expected but more besides. That may, as Jesus put it, involve offering our cloak as well as our coat, but this should be done in a spirit of affirmation rather than denial, of taking on instead of giving up.

So what does that mean in practice? The possibilities are endless. Maybe God is simply asking you, if you haven't done so already, to commit yourself to Christ. Perhaps it's time you took on that extra responsibility in your church, responded to that sense of calling you've repeatedly pushed aside, or played a more active part within the life of your fellowship. On the other hand, the extra mile for you may involve nothing overtly religious at all, the call instead being to get more involved in your local community, help out a neighbour, support some cause, spend more time with your family, show concern to a friend, help out where needed – the sort of things, in other words, that Jesus spoke of in his parable of the sheep and goats: serving him through serving others. None of us can meet every need, but we can all do something, and maybe this Lent the time has come to take on that little bit more. Is that what God is saying to you?

Group activity

'Something extra' (see Appendix 1)

Music

'I give my work to you, Lord' from *Awakening in Love* by Margaret Rizza

Prayer of intercession

Lord Jesus Christ,
    servant of all,
    hear our prayer for those who, in ways large and small,
    offer their own forms of service.
We pray for those in national and local government:
    the prime minister and cabinet, politicians and councillors;
    those in the caring professions:
    GPs, hospital staff, social workers, emergency services,
    clergy, aid workers;
    those involved in education and research:
    teachers, lecturers, professors, scientists;
    those in service industries:

office workers, shop assistants and civil servants;
those bringing practical gifts:
builders, engineers, plumbers and electricians,
factory workers, mechanics, road sweepers and refuse collectors;
those at home:
raising children or caring for loved ones;
each of these, and so many others,
using their gifts to contribute to others.
Above all we pray for those who voluntarily do that little bit extra,
beyond what is asked or expected of them,
freely giving of their time, skills, energy or resources
in order to serve a cause or community close to their heart.
Equip, sustain and encourage all in the service they offer
and grant that their contribution may be recognised and valued.
Amen.

Reading

As they continued on their way, he entered a certain village, where a woman called Martha welcomed him into her home. She had a sister called Mary, who sat at the Lord's feet, listening to his words. Martha, however, was preoccupied with her many tasks; so she came to him and asked, 'Lord, doesn't it matter to you that my sister has left me to do all the work by myself? Tell her to lend a hand.' But the Lord answered, 'Martha, Martha, you are fretting and distracted by many things, but only one thing really matters. Mary has chosen that more important thing, and it will not be taken away from her.'
Luke 10:38-42

Further thoughts

OK, let's get stuck in! You could be forgiven for thinking, from what I've said earlier, that this is how I view the ideal response to Lent, but the story of Martha and Mary counsels caution, for wasn't

Martha doing just that: rolling her sleeves up and getting down to business while her sister lazed around doing nothing? It certainly looks that way at first sight, but, of course, this incident has a deeper message, reminding us that we can be too busy for our own good, a focus on deeds alone, however well intentioned, being counterproductive. Mary understood that there's a time and place for everything, and that, unless we're careful, we can become so preoccupied with service that we've no time to pause and ponder, to make time for what God is saying to us. If we fall into that trap, then all the activity in the world, no matter how well intended, will count for nothing.

Taking things on, then, is potentially as open to abuse as giving them up. Like giving things up, it can be an attempt to earn our salvation or to make us feel good, about winning God's blessing or enjoying the esteem of others. And it too can become a case of works rather than faith, actions becoming more important than devotion, even to the point of replacing it altogether. Lent reminds us of the importance of making time and space for God, putting him first in our lives, seeking his guidance, and recognising our dependence on him for all we do and are. Forget that, and our attempts to go the extra mile, far from honouring God, may end up leading us from him. Get it right, and new avenues will open naturally for us, opportunities to take on new tasks – together with the strength to do them – in grateful response and joyful worship.

Prayer

Living God,
    remind us of the positive side of Lent:
    the opportunities it presents,
    possibilities it opens up
    and response it invites.
Instead of dwelling on what we *can't* do,
    help us to focus on what we *can*,
    on the way we might better use our gifts,

express your love,
offer our service
and do your will.
Show us what you would have us do,
    and equip us gladly to do it,
        through Jesus Christ our Lord.
Amen.

Meditation of a listener to Jesus

'Don't go *one* mile,' he said, 'but *two*.'
Not that hard a challenge, you might think,
    certainly not earth-shattering,
    but for me those words of Jesus opened up new horizons,
    a fresh and almost frightening perspective on what it means to
    serve him.
You see, up till then I'd thought of faith in terms of sacrifice and
    self-denial –
  · avoid this,
    don't do that,
    give up such and such –
    but suddenly here was another angle,
    a different approach,
    it no longer being about what we *can't* do but what we *can*,
    about humbly, willingly, even joyfully taking on that little bit
    extra,
    more than anyone could ask or expect.
It sounded simple,
    but I soon found it wasn't,
    my natural inclination being to do less, not more,
    to take the easy rather than hard path,
    the way that offers the greatest reward for the least effort.
Yet that was no longer an option,
    for there were so many ways I could go that extra mile –

responsibilities I could take on,
jobs that needed doing,
care I could show,
support offer,
help extend,
comfort give,
gifts use,
time commit . . .
and so it went on,
and on.
It had been easy up till then, I realise that now:
a fast here,
sacrifice there –
you know the sort of thing –
and it was done,
life afterwards back to normal.
Walking the way of Christ is different,
asking for more,
much more,
but remember this:
whatever *we* may do beyond the call of duty,
for him or for others,
it's as nothing compared with what *he* has done,
and continues to do each day,
for us.

Closing music

Sing together, or play a recording of, the hymn 'Saviour, thy dying love'.

Final thought

Give me a faithful heart,
likeness to thee,
that each departing day
henceforth may see
some work of love begun,
some deed of kindness done,
some wanderer sought and won –
something for thee.

Blessing

Go with us, Lord,
   that we may go with you.
Work in us,
   that we may work for you.
Speak to us,
   that we may speak of you.
Live in us,
   that we may live through you.
Amen.

Session 5
Over and done with

Opening music

Sing together, or play a recording of, the hymn 'And can it be'.

Setting the scene

And can it be that I should gain
an interest in the Saviour's blood?
Died he for me, who caused his pain?
For me, who him to death pursued?
Amazing love! how can it be
that thou, my God, should die for me!

All too easily we can turn the emphasis of the gospel from positive to negative, an affirmation of forgiveness to a brooding on guilt, but, of course, if we do that we have no gospel at all – nothing to share and still less to celebrate. As Charles Wesley reminds us in that lovely hymn, the Christian message stands or falls not on anything *we* might do but on what God has *done*.

Opening prayer

Gracious God,
    unfold your word to us
    and thrill us afresh with the knowledge
    of what you have done for us in Christ:
    the love you have shown,
    victory won,
    evil defeated
    and promise given.

Help us to grasp the full wonder of what that all means,
    so that its truth may shape everything we think, say and do,
    the people we are and the lives we live,
    through Jesus Christ our Lord.
Amen.

Readings

You, who were dead in your sins and the uncircumcision of your flesh, he has brought to life with him, having forgiven us all our sins, cancelling the debt written against us in the ledger, with all its legal requirements, irrevocably doing away with it by nailing it to the cross.
Colossians 2:13-14

I am convinced that nothing can separate us from Christ's love. Neither death nor life, nor angels nor demons, nor the present nor the future, nor any powers, nor height nor depth nor anything else in all creation, will ever be able to separate us from the love of God that is ours in Christ Jesus our Lord.
Romans 8:38-39

First thoughts

When it comes to the subject of endings, few words are more often quoted than those of Kenneth Wolstenholme, commentating on the 1966 World Cup Final between England and West Germany. 'They think it's all over,' he exclaimed, as fans, believing the match had ended, spilled exuberantly on to the pitch. And then, as Geoff Hurst hammered the ball from distance into the top of the German net to complete a remarkable hat-trick, came the immortal line, 'It *is now!*'

Nearly two thousand years earlier a very different scenario was unfolding, in which once again things seemed to be all over, only this time it was a human life, not a football match, at issue. Outside the walls of Jerusalem a man gasped in agony as he was nailed to a cross, groaned in anguish as his life ebbed slowly away, and for his followers not just his life but also the dreams and faith they had invested in appeared at an end, any remaining shreds of hope laid to rest as they watched him cut down and sealed in a tomb. Only, of course, subsequent events were to prove otherwise, for three days later was to come news of an empty tomb, of Jesus alive, and then, most special of all, the joy of meeting him face to face, experiencing his presence once more by their sides. Defeat was victory; what had looked like the end was in fact a new beginning.

Yet, though they had failed to understand it, something *was* finished that day, over and done with: not the life of Jesus, but the power of evil, the hold of death, the estrangement of God from humankind. That's what God had dealt with in Christ – through his death and resurrection dealing a body blow to whatever denies his love and thwarts his purpose. True, it doesn't always look like it – indeed, all too much in life seems sometimes to suggest the opposite, evil appearing as strong as ever, hatred just as powerful, suffering equally common and death still all too real. Millions continue to suffer in a world scarred by greed, intolerance, hatred, exploitation, terrorism and war, as if the traumas of natural disaster and personal tragedy were not enough already. Yet, as Christians we believe, despite appearances, that good will finally triumph, love emerge victorious, life conquer death. Why? Because the testimony of the Apostles and generations of believers to the living presence of Christ through his Spirit rings true in our hearts. Though evil may still have its day, we believe its wings have been clipped. Though all creation groans together awaiting its final consummation, we look forward to a time when God's purpose will be fulfilled and his love be all in all. As Paul puts it in those wonderful words to the Romans (8:38-39): 'I am convinced that nothing can separate us from Christ's love. Neither death nor life, nor angels nor demons, nor the present nor the future, nor any powers, nor height nor depth nor anything else in all creation, will ever be able to separate us from the love of God that is ours in Christ Jesus our Lord.'

Group activity

'I've started so I'll finish' (see Appendix 1)

Music

'Surely he hath borne our griefs' from Handel's *Messiah*

Prayer of intercession

To those, Lord, oppressed by hatred,
   living in the shadow of violence and terror,
   bring courage to hope and work for a better world,
   assured that love will triumph.

To those oppressed by evil,
   denied the rights we take for granted
   by injustice, corruption, greed and exploitation,
   bring courage to hope and work for a better world,
   assured that good will win through.

To those oppressed by suffering,
   broken by disease,
   tormented by pain,
   stunted by malnutrition,
   crushed by heartache and heartbreak,
   bring courage to hope and work for a better world,
   assured that light will shine again.

To those oppressed by death,
  mourning a loved one,
  tending the dying,
  wrestling with terminal illness,
  or simply coming to terms with their mortality,
  bring courage to hope and work for a better world,
  assured that life will blossom anew.

To all, Lord, may the knowledge of what you've done in Christ
  inspire faith and trust in what is yet to be,
  by his grace.
Amen.

Reading

I do not understand why I act as I do. For I end up doing what I hate rather than what I want to do. Instead of the good I wish to do, I do evil. Now if I do what I'd rather not, it can no longer be I that do it, but must be the sin that dwells within me. I find it to be a law that whenever I intend to do good, evil is there as well, for, while I delight deep within in the law of God, I see a different law in my body that battles with the law of my mind, holding me captive to the law of sin that dwells in my members. What a wretched man I am! Who will deliver me from this body of death? Thanks be to God through Jesus Christ our Lord!

There is, then, no condemnation now for those in Christ Jesus, because the law of the Spirit of life has set us free from the law of sin and death. God has accomplished what the Law, due to our flawed human nature, could never achieve. Through sending his own Son, bearing the weakness of human flesh, he has decisively dealt with our sin, condemning and doing away with it once and for all.

Romans 7:15, 19-25; 8:1-3

Further thoughts

Done, but not yet dusted – in terms of suffering and evil that seems to be the only way to make sense of what God has achieved for us in Christ, the triumph of the cross still awaiting its final consummation. But in another sense the victory he has won is much more immediate, not consigned to the distant future but ours to enjoy here and now. And nowhere is the substance of that spelt out more clearly than in chapters 7 and 8 of Paul's letter to the Romans. Paul begins there by pouring out his frustration over his failure to serve Christ as he would like, his best intentions repeatedly foundering on the rocks of human fallibility. 'I do not understand it,' he says, unable to make sense of his weakness, the way, time and again, he longs to do one thing but ends up doing completely the opposite. Had this ended when he became a Christian? No, he is still vulnerable to temptation, just as we are, weakness and wrongdoing remaining all too much a part of us, however committed we may be. So what's different? What cause is there to hope, let alone good news to share? The answer, says Paul, is very simple – indeed, almost too simple, too straightforward to credit. 'Who will deliver me from this body of death? Thanks be to God through Jesus Christ our Lord!'

In God's eyes, Paul joyfully declares, our sins are paid for once and for all, nailed to the cross, whatever mistakes, faults or failings we may have been guilty of obliterated as though they had never been. Yes, they may have repercussions in the present, just as our former way of life continues to intrude into the new, but in Christ God offers free and full forgiveness. As the first letter of Peter puts it: 'In order to put us right with God, Christ irreversibly died for our sins, a blameless life offered on behalf of sinners' (1 Peter 3:18a). Or to use the words of Hebrews 10:10: 'Because Jesus irrevocably offered his body in accordance with God's will, we are all cleansed from our sins.'

Here is the truth we celebrate as Christians: that if we acknowledge our mistakes and are truly sorry, we can put them behind us and start again, for in God's eyes that's already done. So whatever else you do this Lent, don't turn it into a time of hard labour, doing penance, punishing yourself for past mistakes or present weaknesses. Don't waste it agonising over your faults and struggling desperately to live in such a way that you might somehow do enough to earn pardon and deserve blessing. Not only is that road doomed to failure but it is also a waste of time, for what needs doing has been done already. The debt is cleared, the price paid, the slate wiped clean. God loves you and bids you welcome as you are. Forgiveness is ours for the asking – we need only to reach out and receive.

Prayer

Merciful and gracious God,
   remind us, should we forget,
   of what you have done for us in Christ –
   of the forgiveness you freely offer,
   welcome you daily extend
   and victory you achieved through the cross.
Save us from brooding over our mistakes,
   allowing the past to overshadow the present
   or struggling through life bearing a burden of guilt,
   and, whatever we may face,
   save us also from despair,
   either of ourselves or the situations that confront us.
Assure us of your continuing pardon,
   and, despite all that conspires against it,
   of the ultimate triumph of your love,
   through Jesus Christ our Lord.
Amen.

Meditation of a church member in Rome

Over and done with?
The penalty paid,
  our sins forgiven?
Ridiculous, I thought,
  for it went against everything I'd been taught from childhood,
  my whole understanding of what God required.
Surely there were rituals to observe and rules to adhere to,
  prescribed procedures designed to atone for our faults
  and forestall judgement.
So what was this about God having done it all for us,
  cancelling the debt,
  clearing the record,
  as though our sins could be dealt with once and for all,
  as if they'd never been?
It just didn't feel right not having to perform some ceremony,
  make some sacrifice,
  before forgiveness could be possible,
  yet that, according to Paul, is what God offers:
  full and free forgiveness,
  no strings attached.
And I tell you what, I'm beginning to feel he may be right after all,
  for I've seen lives changed beyond recognition,
  both Jews as well as Gentiles,
  hearts and minds previously hostile to God won over,
  filled with love, joy, trust, hope,
  and, more striking than anything,
  a sense of being at one with God,
  at peace in a way I long to share.
And who's helped to make it all possible?
None other than Paul himself –
  the man who hated and persecuted the Church,
  vowing never to rest until he'd stamped it out,
  hunting down every last one of those
  who walk the way of Christ.

Through one such as him God has made known his love,
  working in ways I scarcely believe
  among those I least expected.
Over and done with?
Forgiven?
Restored?
I still find it hard to swallow,
  hard to believe God could go as far as that,
  yet I found it hard to imagine he could change people
  even a fraction,
  let alone as completely as he has,
  so maybe,
  just maybe,
  it's not so ridiculous, after all.

Closing music

Sing together, or play a recording of, the hymn 'To God be the glory!'

Final thought

To God be the glory! Great things he has done!
So loved he the world that he gave us his Son;
who yielded his life an atonement for sin,
and opened the life-gate that all may go in.

Blessing

Risen Lord,
    may your faithfulness be echoed in our commitment,
    your love reflected in our hearts,
    and your victory be enacted in our lives,
    whatever demeans, defiles, denies or destroys being overcome.
So lead us each day into fullness of life,
    through your saving grace.
Amen.

Session 6
It's only just begun

Opening music

Sing together, or play a recording of, the hymn 'New every morning is the love'.

Setting the scene

New every morning is the love
our wakening and uprising prove;
through sleep and darkness safely brought,
restored to life and power and thought.

So begins the great hymn by John Keble, and his words perfectly set the scene for the final theme of this book: the new beginnings God offers us each day and for all eternity.

Opening prayer

Eternal God,
    remind us, as we begin our session,
    that each moment with you is a fresh start,
    every day full of promise.
Speak to us of the forgiveness you extend,
    the strength you impart,
    the peace you promise
    and the fulfilment you give –
    ours daily to receive and celebrate –
    but, above all, speak of the life you offer,

immeasurable and overflowing,
poured out now and for all eternity,
and in that gift may we find joy now
and hope for the future,
assured of all that yet awaits us by your grace.
Amen.

Reading

I want to know Christ and the power of his resurrection and what
it means to participate in his sufferings through identifying with
him in his death, if, through that, I may somehow attain to the
resurrection from the dead. Not that I have already achieved this or
reached such a goal, but I endeavour continually to make it my own,
just as Christ Jesus has made me his own. Friends, I do not claim
to have yet secured it for myself; but what I do is this: forgetting
what is past and straining forward to what is yet in store, I strive to
reach the goal of the prize of God's heavenly call in Christ Jesus.
Philippians 3:10-14

First thoughts

The more we learn, it is sometimes said, the more we realise how
little we actually know. It's true, isn't it? The world is full of
people who, on casual acquaintance with a subject, consider
themselves qualified to make authoritative pronouncements, while
those blessed with deeper understanding are far more cautious,
openly acknowledging how much remains to be explored. For all
the advances of modern science and technology, these gaps in our
knowledge are increasingly recognised, every discovery opening up
yet new horizons, areas of research previously not even considered.
A hundred years ago, chemists, biologists and physicists believed
they had more or less cracked just about everything worth
discovering; today we realise we've only just begun to scratch
the surface.

Does that same humility characterise our approach to discipleship? It should do, because if God is who we say he is – before all, within all and over all – then we are talking about the greatest wonder, deepest mystery and profoundest truth imaginable, a reality that stretches our minds to the limit and far beyond. Yes, he has made himself known to us in Christ, through him revealing his grace and glory in human form, but, as the Apostle Paul takes pains to stress, for now we see but in part, at best as though looking through a smoked- or frosted-glass window. And if that was true for Paul, with his amazing faith, unparalleled enthusiasm, enormous commitment and wealth of experience, how much more is it the case for us? However long we have been a Christian, however much we have learnt of Christ, we are all just beginners, wrestling with the ABC of faith rather than exhausting its riches. We may know the Bible back to front and the gospel inside out – no matter, we are still novices at the business of discipleship. Indeed, most of us, truth be told, have barely even crossed the starting line, time for God crowded out by other concerns, prayer and reflection pushed to the sidelines, spiritual growth taken for granted. And then we wonder why faith starts to falter, no longer as vibrant or meaningful as it once seemed.

Lent reminds us that commitment is a journey rather than destination, a path stretching out before us rather than goal reached. It calls us to recognise our need to go forward, to explore fresh horizons and chart new territory; in short, to recommit ourselves to a continuing adventure of faith. It offers a window of opportunity that we cannot afford to waste.

Group activity

'We've only just begun' (see Appendix 1)

Music

'Resurrection song' from *Sacred Pathway* by Keith Duke

Prayer of intercession

Creator God,
   we bring you the broken places and people of our world,
   so many situations and lives where hope has been crushed
   and the future seems irretrievably bleak:
   countries and communities battered by natural disaster,
   scarred by division,
   racked by poverty and injustice;
   individuals numbed by bereavement,
   brought low by illness, injury or disease,
   shattered by the breakdown of relationships
   or the collapse of dreams.
Circle them with your love
   and, in your mercy, bring new beginnings,
   fresh vision –
   the courage to look forward again
   and to rebuild not only bricks and mortar
   but also broken lives –
   restoring faith,
   rekindling hope,
   reviving hearts and minds,
   through Jesus Christ our Lord.
Amen.

Reading

Listen and I will tell you a mystery! Not all of us will die, but we will all be changed, in a flash, in the blink of an eye, at the last trumpet. For the trumpet will sound, and the dead will be raised imperishable, and we will be changed. For this ephemeral body must put on an eternal body, and this mortal body must put on immortality. When this is done, then the words of the saying will be fulfilled: 'Death has been swallowed up by victory. Where is your victory, death? Where is your sting?' Death's sting is sin, and

sin's power lies in the law. Give thanks, then, to God who gives us the victory, through our Lord Jesus Christ.
1 Corinthians 15:51-57

Music

Play a brief snippet (i.e. the first few bars) of The Carpenters' song 'We've only just begun'.

Further thoughts

Back in 1970 The Carpenters had a song in the charts titled 'We've only just begun'. The upbeat title masked a tragic irony, for beneath the surface all was not well with lead singer Karen Carpenter. Just a few years later, in 1974, and aged just 24, she was rushed to hospital, her health undermined by the slimming disease, anorexia, and nine years later, following a cardiac arrest, she was dead. Her story cruelly illustrates both the beauty and tragedy of life, its promise yet pathos, triumph yet tragedy. Our brief span on earth offers so much that is special, so much joy and loveliness, yet along-side it lurks the spectre of disillusionment, heartbreak, suffering and death, the knowledge that in this life nothing lasts for ever. What's begun today is all too swiftly over tomorrow.

Yet if the title of that song may be inappropriate in terms of this world, it offers nonetheless a perfect summary of life in Christ, a simple but wonderful synopsis of the hope at the heart of the gospel, for its message is surely, above all else: we've only just begun! Whoever we are and whatever we face, God daily holds out the prospect of a fresh start, new horizons beckoning us onwards. Not only is he always willing to forgive and forget, putting the past forever behind us, but he also offers inner strength, a sense of purpose and true fulfilment, each moment through him holding fresh promise, untold possibilities.

But hang on, I hear you say: that's all very well when life is good, but what about those facing harder times, those for whom the present offers anything but pleasure and the future seems bleak? What promise is there for the terminally ill or chronically suffering, the old and infirm, the bereaved or broken in body, mind and spirit? And what of those for whom each day is a battle for survival, their lives overshadowed by famine and disease, poverty and oppression, war and hatred? How far does it make sense to talk of new beginnings in the light of their experience?

It's a fair question and one that would be hard to answer if our hope was based in this world only, the facts seeming to fly in the face of faith. Yes, we could speak of inner peace, of God offering comfort and reassurance in times of crisis, but what would those amount to if they were the end of the story, blotted out by death? Quite simply, not enough. But our conviction as Christians is that death is not the end but a new beginning, a turning over from one chapter to the next. That, and that alone, is the context in which faith is rooted, the promise that turns what would otherwise be empty delusion into confident trust and eager expectation. We do not know the ins and outs, yet we believe that after death comes resurrection, after this life, life to come, after the grave a kingdom that will never end, after this world a new heaven and earth. Take that away and, as Paul reminds us, we are of all people most to be pitied. Recognise its truth, however, and with him we can joyfully declare, 'Death has been swallowed up by victory. Where is your victory, death? Where is your sting? Give thanks to God who gives us the victory, through our Lord Jesus Christ.'

Who can say what life will bring: joy or sorrow, pleasure or pain, success or failure, delight or disillusionment? We taste both its sweetness and bitterness, faith giving no guarantee of the first nor exemption from the second. Yet, whatever it holds, we know that nothing will ever be able to separate us from the love of God in Christ. So we look forward in faith, aware that, come what may, we've only just begun.

Prayer

Mighty God,
    whatever full stops life appears to bring,
    whatever defeats, disappointments or dead ends
    we come up against,
    teach us never to lose heart
    or to abandon faith in your continuing purpose.
Remind us that you are a God of new beginnings,
    able to take what is and shape what will be,
    bringing advance after reversal,
    gain out of loss,
    sunshine after rain,
    life from dry bones.
Speak, then,
    each day,
    each moment,
    of the fresh start you set before us –
    the opportunities to grasp,
    possibilities to explore
    and wonders to celebrate –
    and remind us that though heaven and earth pass away,
    your kingdom will endure for ever
    and the life you hold in store remain always new,
    through Jesus Christ our Lord.
Amen.

Meditation of the Apostle Paul

They expected me to be afraid,
    I realised that afterwards:
    the three of them –
    Felix, Festus and Agrippa –
    actually thought I'd fear for the future,
    that the prospect of facing death would sway my devotion,
    undermine my commitment to preach the gospel of Christ.

I can understand why, of course,
 because for them life was everything,
 each moment filled with the frantic search for more
 and the dread of losing what they had –
 but how little they knew of me or the things of God.
They could have ended my life then and there if they'd wanted to –
 I'm under no illusions, make no mistake –
 and no doubt, sooner rather than later,
 Caesar or one of his minions will do just that.
But though they can snuff out my body,
 there's one thing they can never touch:
 the awesome and inexpressible gift I've found in Christ:
 life not of this world,
 but kept in heaven,
 holding things in store too wonderful to contemplate,
 greater than I could ever ask or imagine,
 beyond words,
 beyond price.
So yes, I'm well aware that my days are numbered,
 the prospect of execution being more a case of 'when' than 'if',
 but it doesn't scare me,
 still less cause me to question or lose heart,
 for though my earthly journey is nearly at an end,
 life is far from over –
 it has only just begun!

Closing music

Sing together, or play a recording of, the hymn 'One more step along the world we go'.

Final thought

For it's from the old we travel to the new,
keep me travelling along with you.

Blessing

Send us out, Lord, with faith, joy and hope,
    the knowledge of what you have done
    assuring us of all you are doing and will yet do,
    through Jesus Christ our Lord.
Amen.

Appendix 1
Quiz questions

Session 1 – Past history

1. Which royal dynasty came to an end in 1485, and where?
2. Which illness was a vaccine devised for in 1796, and by whom? When was the disease declared officially eradicated?
3. When was the Berlin wall dismantled?
4. Which year saw the first official steps in the end of apartheid?
5. What was finally abolished in Britain in 1833?
6. Which conflict came to an end in 1865?
7. What was officially ended in Britain in 1965, and when was the last recorded case?
8. What ended on 5 September 1666?
9. In which year did decimal currency spell the end in the UK of the old pound, shilling and pence?
10. What was finally achieved on 29 May 1953?

Session 2 – Beginnings and endings

1. Which classic book begins with the words 'It was the best of times, it was the worst of times'?
2. How does T. S. Eliot's famous poem 'The Wasteland' begin?
3. Which play begins with the words 'When shall we three meet again?'? _Macbeth_.
4. Which song begins with the words 'When you're weary, feeling small'? _Bridge over troubled water_
5. How does the Desiderata begin?
6. Which book ends with the words 'After all, tomorrow is another day'? _Gone with the wind_
7. Which book opens with the words 'It is a truth universally acknowledged . . .'?

8. What is the first line of Wordsworth's famous poem about daffodils? *I wandered lonely as a cloud*

9. Which song ends with the words 'and the world will live as one'? *Imagine - John Lennon*

10. Whose last words were reportedly, 'I'm not the least afraid to die'?

Session 3 – Giving it up

1. In which year did Edward VIII give up his throne to marry Wallis Simpson?

2. Whom was Princess Margaret pressurised into giving up, rather than lose her place in the royal succession?

3. Who gave up playing county and Test cricket to focus on a career in the Church?

4. Who sacrificed the chance to win the 100 metres medal at the 1924 Olympics in Paris rather than race on a Sunday? What event did he nonetheless win and which other medal besides a gold?

5. Who gave up his life peerage so that he could serve as a member of parliament?

6. Who gave up food for three weeks in a much publicised fast, later, in 1948, giving up his life?

7. In which Hans Christian Andersen story does the heroine give up her voice to be with her true love?

8. Which illustrious scientist, cleric and theologian gave up a comfortable lifestyle to become a medical missionary, fighting leprosy and sleeping sickness, at Lambaréné in French Equatorial Africa?

9. Who gave up his life rather than compromise his convictions over Henry VIII's marriage to Anne Boleyn?

10. Which Yugoslav gave up the security of teaching in a convent to work among the poorest of the poor?

Session 4 – Something extra

Add letters before each of the following to make a word (or words) that has something to do with beginnings:

1. _ _ _ _WORD
2. _ _ _ _ACE
3. _ _ _AMBLE
4. _ _ _ DEN _ _ _ AGE (two words)
5. _ _ BUT
6. _ _ _ _ _ _IF
7. _ _ TRY
8. _ _ _ _ _ _ RATE
9. _ _ _ _ _ _ _ _ _ ION
10. _ _ _ _ _ ER

Session 5 – I've started so I'll finish

1. Whose 'catchphrase' was 'I've started so I'll finish', and on which programme was it used?
2. Who wrote the famous 'Unfinished Symphony'?
3. Whose colossal six-volume work *The History of the Decline and Fall of the Roman Empire* took 12 years to complete?
4. Whose celebrated work was in fact completed by the composer Franz Süssmayer?
5. Who finally won the Wimbledon Ladies Singles title in 1969 after having been a finalist once and semi-finalist on six previous occasions?
6. What did Lloyd Scott, a former fireman, achieve on 14 April 2002 (wearing a diving suit!)?
7. Which great British cathedral took 74 years to build, work on it starting in 1904 and being completed in 1978?
8. Which celebrated British mathematician contributed to the eventual cracking of the Enigma Code?
9. What was unravelled in 1953, and by whom?
10. What did Fred Davis finally achieve in 1980?

Session 6 – We've only just begun

For this activity, the leader needs to record, in advance, the opening few bars of various well-known pieces of music (10-20 pieces in all). Play these to the group, and see how many can identify the music from the brief snippets heard.

Appendix 2
Quiz answers

Session 1 – Past history

1. The Plantagenets, at the Battle of Bosworth Field
2. The smallpox vaccine was isolated by Edward Jenner, the disease finally being declared eradicated across the world in 1979
3. 1989
4. 1990
5. Slavery
6. The American Civil War
7. The death penalty for murder, Ruth Ellis being the last person to hang in 1955
8. The Great Fire of London
9. 1971
10. Everest was climbed for the first time (by Sherpa Tenzing Norgay and Sir Edmund Hillary)

Session 2 – Beginnings and endings

1. *A Tale of Two Cities* by Charles Dickens
2. 'April is the cruellest month'
3. *Macbeth*
4. 'Bridge over troubled water'
5. 'Go placidly amid the noise and haste . . .'
6. *Gone with the Wind*
7. *Pride and Prejudice*
8. 'I wandered lonely as a cloud'
9. 'Imagine' by John Lennon
10. Charles Darwin

Session 3 – Giving it up

1. 1936
2. Group Captain Peter Townsend
3. David Sheppard
4. Eric Liddell. He finished third in the 200 metres, and then won the 400 metres, setting a new world record of 47.6 seconds in doing so
5. Anthony (Tony) Wedgwood Benn
6. Mahatma Gandhi
7. *The Little Mermaid*
8. Albert Schweitzer
9. Sir Thomas More
10. Mother Teresa

Session 4 – Something extra

1. FOREWORD
2. PREFACE
3. PREAMBLE
4. MAIDEN VOYAGE
5. DEBUT
6. APERITIF
7. ENTRY
8. INAUGURATE
9. INTRODUCTION
10. STARTER

Session 5 – I've started so I'll finish

1. Magnus Magnusson, as the quizmaster on *Mastermind*
2. Franz Schubert
3. Edward Gibbon

4. Mozart, his *Requiem*
5. Ann Jones
6. The slowest ever London Marathon (five days, eight hours and 20 minutes)
7. Liverpool Anglican Cathedral
8. Alan Turing
9. The structure of DNA, by James Watson and Francis Crick
10. He won the World Professional Billiards title at the age of 66, successfully defending it the following year

Session 6 – We've only just begun

For this quiz, of course, you will need to provide your own answers, corresponding to the pieces you have chosen your opening snippets from.

Suggested music resources in this book

CD
1490110

Cassette
1480095

Full Score
1450276
1 84417 052 7

Vocal Score
1450277
1 84417 051 9

Melody Edition
1450297
1 84417 158 2

CD
1490145

Cassette
1480096

Full Score
1450307
1 84417 217 1

Vocal Score
1450308
1 84417 276 7

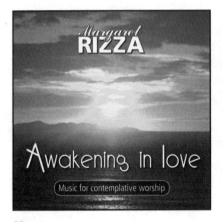

CD
1490141

Full Score
1450312
1 84417 229 5

Vocal Score
1450313
1 84417 230 9

CD
1490024

Full Score
1400147
1 84003 033 X

Vocal Score
1450090
1 84003 057 7

Melody Edition
1400148
1 84003 061 5

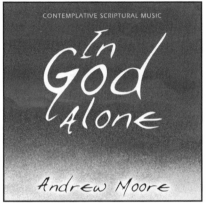

CD
1490123
Full Score
1450295
1 84417 156 6

CD
1490175